BRITAIN'S HERITAGE

Corgi Toys

Mick Overton

AMBERLEY

Acknowledgements

The author would like to thank everyone who has provided him with images, information and checked details that have gone into this book, especially Vicky Weal and Simon Smith at Vectis Auctions Limited. Also Simon Phillips, Martin Rayner and Christopher Cousins. Special thanks to Nick Jones and Nick Wright for choosing the author to write this book! And for inspiration and original source of much information, thanks to Marcel Van Cleemput, Designer of Corgi Toys and author of *The Great Book of Corgi*, this writer's die-cast hero since buying the book in 2001.

Every attempt has been made to seek permission for copyright material used in this book. However, if we have inadvertently used copyright material without permission/ acknowledgement we apologise and we will make the necessary correction at the first opportunity.

Cover image: Corgi brightened up their box design on 1959 by adding yellow areas and changing their shade of blue to the now-familiar corporate colours. The rarest and most valuable Corgi Land Rover issue is this France-only #416S (S for added wire suspension) Touring Secours, which was sold for £1,800 by Vectis Auctions in July 2018.

First published 2019

Amberley Publishing
The Hill, Stroud
Gloucestershire, GL5 4EP

www.amberley-books.com

ISBN 978 1 4456 8808 4 (paperback)
ISBN 978 1 4456 8809 1 (ebook)

British Library Cataloguing in Publication Data.
A catalogue record for this book is available from the British Library.

Printed in the UK.

Appointed GPSR EU Representative: Easy Access System Europe Oü, 16879218
Address: Mustamäe tee 50, 10621, Tallinn, Estonia
Contact Details: gpsr.requests@easproject.com, +358 40 500 3575

Contents

1 Introduction: In the Beginning 4

2 Big Cars 1956–72 9

3 Husky – The Pocket Money Toys 29

4 Corgi Rockets and Juniors – with Whizzwheels 35

5 Bigger Cars 1972–83 53

6 What Next? 62

1
Introduction: In the Beginning

Did You Know?

Top Gear's James May regards the Corgi James Bond Goldfinger Aston Martin DB5 as 'the most significant car ever', beating all full-sized cars! It was awarded the first ever 'Toy of the Year' title in 1966 and sold over 4 million examples by 1969, with many millions more since in five incarnations (1/45, two 1/43 models, 1/36, Husky/Juniors). This toy car remains in production today as a Corgi, having been enjoyed by tens of milions of children over the past fifty-three years. James May recognises its culture-changing impact on the two generations of children that grew up with them as mechanical marvels shooting the baddie out of the roof (only to lose him!) and who now, aged thirty-five to sixty, have brought about the modern classic car movement as well as contributing to the survival of Aston Martin, who still make cars with DB5 design cues and are now even putting the DB5 back into production.

Established Northampton-based metal toy maker The Mettoy Company Limited created Corgi Toys. They first went on sale nationwide in the UK from 9 July 1956, shipped from a new factory in Wales located in an unemployment blackspot with government encouragement. Stocks were also supplied to interested European, Commonwealth and North American retailers in order to be on sale worldwide in the same month, July 1956.

The Corgi Toys name was first suggested by director Henry Ullmann, the son of Mettoy's founder, during 1955. The recently crowned Queen Elizabeth II kept the sturdy Welsh Corgi breed of dog in the public eye as well as adding perceived prestige; thus it was a very compelling choice to brand the world's best-quality sturdy toy cars, fit for everyman's little prince, with a name that also reflected that they were made in Wales. The concept behind the new brand was to make a competititively priced, while at the same time more luxurious, range of diecast toys that targeted as well as expanded the market established by the robust but basic Dinky Toys (and the American brand Tootsie Toys) twenty years earlier.

The business that became The Mettoy Company was founded by Philipp Ullmann in 1933 when he moved to the UK from Germany, having already worked in the toy industry for twenty-one years, latterly owning his own company there, Tipp & Co. Six months later Tipp & Co.'s Arthur Katz joined him from Germany to build up Mettoy – the name coming from combining the first three letters of 'metal' with toy, tinplate toys being their primary products.

Mettoy had been producing premium priced CASTOYS-branded diecast clockwork and pull-back motor vehicles in the UK, primarily for Marks & Spencers shops, since 1948 (an exclusive relationship which continued into the 1980s) but with the diecasting subcontracted to the Birmingham Aluminium Casting Company. The 6-inch-long Castoys van number 870 was produced in different liveries, reflecting Mettoy's product planning, which favoured tooling with obvious multiple uses and pre-dated the Corgi Toys brand, and which was no doubt inspired by the Dinky 28 series of vans first introduced in 1934.

In 1950 Mettoy introduced the true forerunners of the Corgi brand, promoted as Mettoy Playthings and catalogued as the 'Miniature numbers' range. These seven products included both a 3-inch and a circa 1/43 scale Rolls-Royce plus Standard Vanguard models, all motorised but comparable scalewise to the Corgi and Husky/Corgi Juniors ranges.

When in 1953 zinc alloy diecasting expert Howard Fairbairn quit the Birmingham Aluminium Casting Company to join Mettoy as a director, the company acquired the in-house focus to create a superior rival to Dinky Toys as envisioned by Henry Ullmann. Howard Fairbairn had been the liason man for the Birmingham Aluminium Casting Co. with Dinky Toys' Binns Road factory for the production of aluminium Dinky Toys so he already had an inside perspective of the major player in the diecast toy business. He was given the sole power to approve or veto any proposed Corgi toy from the beginning until 1970, when a design and marketing committee of between six and fourteen persons took over this responsibilty.

Chief designer of the Mettoy Corgi models from the beginning in 1956 to the end in 1983, Marcel Van Cleemput, joined Mettoy on 1 January 1954.

Design work on the launch range for the yet to be named brand began in April 1955. Plans were to produce an initial seven saloon cars, two sports cars, a van (both with and without side windows) and a truck (with choice of dropside and refrigerator bodies). The chosen subjects were all popular modern vehicles on British roads as well as current showroom representatives of the major brands in the British motor industry. Tool-making for the diecast moulds was subcontracted to three German companies that had the skills and could deliver quality at a price not readily available in house at Mettoy yet.

In order to compete successfully with Dinky and European diecast not just by matching prices, Mettoy came up with two innovative selling points. Firstly, all models would have

These Mettoy tinplate models from the 1930s to the 1950s illustrate the company's first toy focus and were auctioned by Vectis.

Here are both 1/43 and 3-inch scale models of the Rolls-Royce from Mettoy Playthings' Miniature Numbers series. Note that the car in the centre has bumpers that slide inwards, changing the gear from forward to reverse and vice versa when the clockwork key wound-up car hits a wall.

These prints from chief designer Marcel Van Cleemput's personal archive were among many auctioned by Vectis and show him at work.

clear plastic windows promoted by the use of the slogan 'The First with Windows'. Secondly, they would offer a premium priced alternative colour version of each diecast model fitted with a small pull-back motor already commonplace in the pressed tinplate toycars previously produced by Mettoy since 1936.

These pull-back motors featured a flywheel designed to be fully loaded when the car was pulled back 2 feet and intended to take the car 'thirty-five to forty feet' on release depending upon the weight of the casting according to Marcel Van Cleemput. The motorised diecast toys were to prove a total flop – a high proportion of cars could not travel in a straight line, motors wore out surprisingly quickly, picking up dust and hairs, and they appeared underpowered compared to the best clockwork alternatives. Design and performance of these pull-back motors were constrained given the toy's weight and the internal space of each diecast model. Compared to a hand-pushed basic Corgi, the price premium put motorised versions at a huge disadvantage because they were sold alongside outwardly similar standard Corgi Toys.

The established Dinky Toys cars were scaled near 1/43 in such a way that one-size wheels fitted all models in close to realistic proportions; in addition, each model appeared in a similar size to offer children equal value for money because all cars were sold at the same price. New Corgi Toys would also be scaled to all use the same size wheels; however, there was a specific design requirement for a semblance to real life scale and perspective so that the largest cars in real life were also the largest cars in the Corgi range when toys were lined up, even if the widths on some models ended up being exaggerated to achieve a child's-eye perspective of the real vehicles. The earliest trucks to join the range were scaled at around 1/55 in proportion to use the same wheel hubs as the 1956 car range, although in some cases with fatter rubber tyres fitted.

Corgi Toys models were launched at a standard wholesale price, enabling shops to charge retail prices of around 3 shillings apiece for all basic cars without motors. These fourteen new Corgi Toys launch castings launched as twenty-four different catalogue numbers,

Sold by Vectis, this engineering prototype of the motorised Corgi #200 Consul fitted with working steering survived in designer Marcel Van Cleemput's collection, demonstrating that steering mechanisms were evaluated but rejected in 1956 (but later introduced on the 1960s VW Beetle and Austin A60 Cambridge).

The Mettoy Karrier Bantam CWS truck was made in 1955 exclusively for the CWS soft drinks company. This example was sold by Vectis Auctions Ltd for £1,100 in 2016. In January 1957 this tooling was improved with Corgi wheels and the Corgi name added to the baseplate to be manufactured and sold in blue livery as Corgi #455. It was the sole Mettoy-branded product rebranded as a Corgi.

including both standard and motorised models, that were all initially released in authentic manufacturers' colours as a key selling point. However, Mettoy quickly learned that drab authentic colours were not a positive selling point, so they were replaced in production by brighter toy colours including metallics and two-tones. Management soon realised that the Dinky pricing strategy of one price fits all cars would not enable Corgi Toys to innovate so new models were soon priced on an individual actual cost plus basis. This resulted in the newest, superior models costing more than older, less sophisticated toys with Corgi's evolving engineering skills and imaginative use of plastics ahead of their competitors.

2

Big Cars 1956–72

These playroom time-served old Consuls are in authentic Ford colours and, being Corgi's first model cast, show the charm of collecting playworn toys. The blue car is motorised first issue #200M while the beige car is the basic #200 Corgi, both from 1956.

The new Corgi Toys range was launched with plans to add two more new models per month from the beginning of 1957 and into the forseeable future. The first Corgi car to be selected and tooled up was the 1951–56 #200 Ford Consul – a very popular modern British postwar family saloon that Mettoy already had manufactured in plastic from 1954 but much larger than 1/43 scale. Its most direct high street rival, the Austin A50 Cambridge, was the second car chosen. The other five saloon cars chosen included one each from five more of the most popular British family car brands – the Morris Cowley, Vauxhall Velox, Rover 90, Hillman Husky and Riley Pathfinder. There were two sports cars, a Triumph TR2 and a big Austin Healy. Six versions of the practical Bedford CA van were included in the initial twenty-four models and they were to be the first of many liveries applied to both the dormobile and closed van versions of this tooling. Two versions of the Commer TS3 truck completed the whole launch lineup, of which in 1956 alone a total of over 1,300,000 Corgi Toys were shipped to shops and wholesalers by Mettoy. Significant quantities of early production cars made in 1956 were completed with vac-formed glazing, which was thinner, clearer and flexible compared to the standard hard injection moulded windows – they look better than the standard models but don't attract any price premium.

The Corgi Model Club was formed by the company back in those early days in 1956 to promote the new brand among children and encourage interest as well as anticipation of planned new releases. This continued well into the 1970s, offering the Corgi Model Club newsletter magazine in addition to the membership certificate and club badge even as the upper age limit at which boys normally purchased toy cars declined from sixteen in the 1950s to eight in the mid-1970s.

Corgi Collector catalogues were introduced early in 1957 and included artists' impressions of approved new castings scheduled for release – they were quickly established as an effective

From the July 1956 launch selection, this 205M Riley Pathfinder is the premium priced motorised issue, as the M on the box discloses. This was arguably the most modern-looking car in the early range even if it took Corgi an extra two years to get the planned police version into shops. (Vectis)

way to make sure children knew the choices available and have been very collectable ever since, in part because they illustrate colours or variations of models which are either very rare or were never released as such because Corgi changed their plans at too short notice for the catalogues to take changes into account.

Corgi began twenty years of regular advertising in lots of childrens' comics in many countries where the toys were sold, although that was the responsibility of the appointed importer for each country outside the UK. Corgi also began experimenting with TV advertising in the UK for the first time using the slogan 'You've seen them on TV – the ones with windows,' although the only really memorable TV adverts Corgi made were for the launch of Corgi Rockets, shown in the UK in 1969–70.

Only one non-luxury British car brand was missing from the 1956 Corgi range, so it was no surprise that a Standard Vanguard became the eighth Corgi saloon car made, along with a ninth, a Jaguar 2.4 Mark 1, at the beginning of 1957. At the same time, the Mettoy diecast Karrier Bantam CWS drinks truck was modified with Corgi wheels and Corgi branding on its base to join the Corgi range as its third truck. An MGA became the third sports car in the catalogue while Stirling Moss's Formula 1 Grand Prix Vanwall became Corgi's first racing car. August 1957 saw Corgi sell their first version of the Land Rover 109, which would in all its issues – which included remaking and updating worn out tooling at least twice – be the first Corgi to sell well over 10 million examples (with the original 1960s tooling exported and revived in China by the new Corgi company to make Vanguards collectables into the new millenium). October 1957 saw the introduction of the first Corgi Major toy, a weighty Bedford S type hauled car transporter in 1/47 scale which was entirely tooled up by Mettoy in their own toolroom using a much larger than before diecasting machine to handle the longer casting. It was more than double the length of a Corgi car at that time and sophisticated too, with the top deck lowering and raising with hydraulic-looking jacks. This became part of the first Corgi gift set alongside four random saloon and sports cars from the range. The final

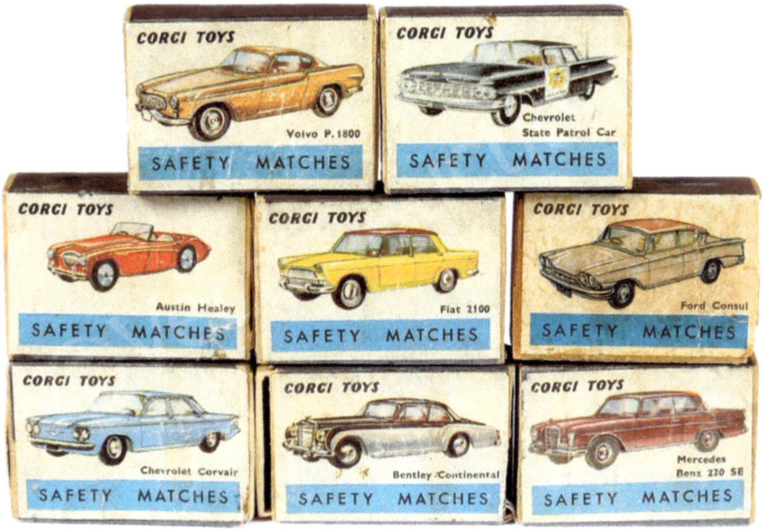

Corgi matches were a clever way to promote the newest Corgi toys in the early 1960s when collecting matchboxes was a popular hobby. This set was sold by Vectis.

new model for 1957 featured Corgi's new standard diecast base in place of cheaper tinplate and was the first foreign car to be modelled: the Citroën DS19. To be fair, though, it was partly British as Citroën had an assembley line in Slough!

1958 marked the first of Marcel Van Cleemput's many experiences of working alongside a motor manufacturer to produce a toy of a new car product to be launched on the same day as the 1:1, in complete secrecy to avoid press leaks. Unfortunately the Rover Road Hawk was cancelled by the manufacturer at a very late stage in November 1958, having been delayed when initially due in showrooms in July 1958. Rover required Corgi to destroy the car moulds and printing plates for the #212 boxes as well as the test models produced – only two castings and one box survived thanks to Marcel Van Cleemput's sense of history. Corgi modelled their own full-size sales promotional display truck, a Smiths custom-bodied Karrier Bantam, as #407 (later #413). However, it failed to obtain approval to ever be sold in the Corgi livery of a prototype from the Marcel Van Cleemput Collection, although the Bedford CA was sold in Corgi colours!

Otherwise, Corgi released a similar mix of new castings in 1958, including futher versions of exisiting tooling. Corgi's first American model, the Studebaker Golden Hawk, was released in February. The Thunderbird guided missile towed by a Land Rover became the first of many military models for years that were regarded as 'The Rocket Age' in May. The long anticipated police version of the 1953–57 Riley Pathfinder was released in June, two years after the plain family car version – alongside its badge engineered twin the Wolseley 6/90, they were the most visible British police cars on the roads in the mid-1950s. A 1/18 scale diecast version of the #150 Vanwall was made exclusively for Marks & Spencers; however, this model was never actually branded as a Corgi although Marcel Van Cleemput has written that with hindsight it should have been! November saw the release of Corgi's first construction model, the Euclid TC12 Dozer – apparently easy to research as the Euclid factory was only 2 miles away from the Mettoy factory in Swansea.

1959 was the year that Corgi introduced bright two-tone paintwork to refresh the first six car castings from 1956 as well as to make new models like the #214 Ford Thunderbird and the Decca mobile airfield radar truck look more attractive to children, in contrast to the often drab

Above: Corgi's original 1956 box designs were very drab, especially when combined with models coloured RAF grey. These Rocket age toys were not huge sellers when new and remain one of the often overlooked segments of the range for modern collectors. (Vectis)

Left: Of all the standard Corgi models given their own product number, the rarest is the #349 Mini Mostest, with mint boxed examples selling for around £1,000 each on the rare occasions that they turn up. Only a few gross were shipped to Denmark and distributed to high-end toy stores there between late 1968 and early 1969. The remaining stock manufactured was destroyed along with the rest of the factory warehouse stock in a fire on Monday 10 March 1969.

colours seen on the local streets. The Massey Ferguson tractor and trailer became the first of the long-lived niche farm models in May. Corgi's final motorised model was the #216M Austin A40, released in June, with final stocks of all remaining motorised models dispatched from the factory warehouse during 1960, thus ending the use of M suffix catalogue and box numbers.

The July release #219 Plymouth Sports Suburban Wagon was the very first closed-roof Corgi to be fitted with vac-formed plastic seats and a moulded steering wheel – its baseplate design shows that it had been changed at a late stage, deleting the now disountinued flywheel motor. Previously only open-top sports cars by both Corgi and Dinky featured seats diecast as part of the body with a separate moulded or cast steering wheel.

Corgi's last 1959 patented design improvement, 'Glidamatic' suspension, was introduced in October on the #222 Renault Floride, launched on the same date that Renault launched the Floride at the 1959 Earl's Court Motor Show. All newly tooled car models from this date were given Glidamatic independent suspension, which comprised two lengths of thin, stiff wire held to the diecast chassis by crimps.

The year ended with all production getting better quality paintwork as conveyer belt flat spray painting was dropped in favour of rotary painting, using castings hung on spinning rods to ensure effective paint coverage of the whole exterior of each casting. Painting under the fins of the new #223 and #220 Chevrolet Impalas had prompted this change. Not to be overlooked, but sadly discontinued after only a few years, was the release of Corgi accessory packs #1460–1464. They were a very clever quality way for children to detail cars with stickers that included numberplates, tax discs, AA and RAC badges, GB plates, L plates, stickers for trucks and patterned foil hubcaps and white wall tyre edges that fitted well on flat Corgi wheel hubs and that still suit these today when owned by adult collectors! 1959 marked the peak production volumes and biggest unit sales figures for rivals Dinky – in all, future years' sales shrank while Corgi still had eight years of growth ahead.

Corgi's big innovation in 1960 featured an opening bonnet, revealing a profile of the engine fitted to the fullsize car – modelled as the #218 Aston Martin DB4. Corgi's first Austin and Morris Minis (#225 and #226) were released in authentic manufacturers' colours – and a Mini remained in the range in later retoolings beyond the end of Mettoy in 1983. Corgi's first London taxi, the #418 Austin FX4, was another model to remain in the range retooled

This group of emergency services cars show the change from first generation box art to second, as well as the use of Corgi accessory stickers for the numberplates and hubcaps on the Zephyr and the tax disc on the Riley. (Vectis)

This box shows the catalogue S suffix, which only applied to the half-dozen castings upgraded to sprung suspension in 1960. Many people have noticed that the design of the Jaguar Mark I seems influenced by the Citroën DS19!

beyond the end of Mettoy. The Bedford CA tooling was updated to reflect the new one-piece windscreen CA body while the Triumph TR2 nose was modified to the new TR3 look – these were the first castings updated to reflect model updates on the streets.

Six S suffix models appeared in catalogues when the Jaguar Mark 1, Citroën DS19, Studebaker Golden Hawk and Ford Thunderbird were upgraded to 1960 standards with seats and steering wheels while motorised baseplate moulds were modified to include Glidamatic crimped stiff wire suspension in place of motor mountings. This distinction (i.e. 208, 208M and 208S for the Jaguar) meant that there would be no confusion with older stocks of motorised or basic versions of the same casting. The 211S Studebaker Golden Hawk was the first of the multitude of Corgi models over the decades to be given a highly appropriate gold chrome vacuum-plated finish to help it sell. And just in time for Christmas shoppers, Major toy #1121 was the first Chipperfield's Circus item, a wonderful circus crane based upon an American Army war surplus truck.

1961 marked the introduction of the #224 Bentley Continental – the casting that raised the bar for the industry and which introduced (glass) jewelled headlamps and rear lights, self-centring steering, chrome-plated grille/bumpers and an opening boot containing a spare tyre, all in a choice of two smart two-tone paint schemes. Corgi's first ever bus came out as #1120, an M1 motorway Midland Red Express coach. The successful gift set range expanded with its first Chipperfields set, which appealed to girls as well as boys. Poor sales results with the Golden Guinea gift set (collectable gold vacuum-plated versions of the Bentley, Consul Classic and Corvair) and the Marks & Spencers 'Trophy' exclusive selection of five collectable 'gold' race cars and sports cars proved rare exceptions to Corgi's usual golden touch choices of those years!

1962 featured the growth of the contents of the flagship Chipperfield's Circus gift set as well as the first Corgi to have a battery and working flashing lights, cleverly engineered to use one bulb and four clear pipes to split that bulb between four lights. Corgi subcontracted

The artwork on all the Chipperfield's Circus gift sets was superb and proved to have significant play value for girls of the 1960s as well as boys, an important Christmas gift marketing consideration! (Vectis)

manufacture of their first handpainted plastic figures (sold separately as well as in the Grand Prix gift set) to a Hong Kong producer and this was standard procedure for almost all handpainted plastic figures ever made for Mettoy. Plastic kits of track and street furniture also started joining the range to add imaginative play value.

The 'Trans-O-Lite' idea was perfected for 1963 without need for a battery on the modified VW van in Toblerone livery, which was the best selling version of the #433, #434 and #441 VW split-screen van models. Although small numbers of promotional issues were made (notably for Dutch coffee-makers), it was a surprise that this icon-to-be toy sold less than one million combined units. The other wizard new gimmicks offered by new '63 Corgi Toys were pop-up jewelled headlamps on the Corvette Stingray (which also featured cost-cutting plastic sprung suspension) and, by a similar principle, a fold-down back seat in the #436 Citroën ID19 Safari and #251 Hillman Imp. The industry bar was raised with opening doors, bonnet and boot combined with suspension, tilting seats, chromed bumpers and jewel headlamps featuring on the November release of the design concept #241 Chrysler Ghia 6.4L. This was a huge seller for Corgi in very smart metallic colours, proving that it was features rather than familiarity from the streets that made children choose one car over another.

In 1964, coinciding with the thirtieth anniversary of the founding of Mettoy, Corgi launched the first of their few Classics models – pre-1930 vintage cars aimed primarily at the Matchbox Models of Yesteryear market segment. Using consistent scale, superb cast details like exhaust pipes and spoked wheels, and authentic paints, there is no doubt these models were far superior to Yesteryears; however, they were also much more costly than Yesteryears and thus failed to secure a significant niche in the market. The 1927 Bentley Le Mans is the most desirable model of this series because it was subsequently tied into popular TV shows

This split-screen VW pickup with canopy is hard to find today. Not many were made because the tooling was modified, turning it into a tow truck with a toolkit. (Vectis)

Corgi's first London Routemaster bus #468 was only made in London Transport red aside from a single short run made in Sydney Australian livery to the order of that importer in the late 1960s. However, this colour trial in Green Line livery with doors belonged to Marcel Van Cleemput and was sold by Vectis after his death. The need to add doors was one reason why it wasn't made like this, although Marcel Van Cleemput never forgot this model because in 1982 the #470 was released in brighter green, based upon the bigger #469 casting without doors!

of the 1960s *The Avengers* and *World of Wooster* (Corgi's first flop in the film/TV genre). February 1964 featured the release of Corgi's first rally car, the #317 Monte Carlo Mini, only weeks after it won the race in January; it was updated in the next three years to reflect further winning Mini Coopers and sold very well. June 1964 saw the delayed release of another long-lived huge seller – Corgi's first London double-decker bus, a superbly designed and finished #468 Routemaster featuring the unique front end of the 1958 prototype RML3 registered SLT 58, suggesting photos and measurements had been taken years earlier! Corgi's out-of-the-box gimmick in the 1964 range was the axle-powered windscreen wiper mechanism on the #247 Mercedes 600 Pullman – it sold almost one million pieces in less than five years; however, its small 1/50 scale meant that it never looked right next to standard Corgis at closer to 1/43 scale and the feature was never used again. The superior Dinky 1/43 scale version of the same car was made in the exact same candy deep red but featured all opening doors, bonnet and boot, remaining in production until 1978.

1965 began with the release of nine existing car/van and three Major truck castings in US Army olive green, approximating vehicles seen on NATO bases throughout Europe. However, they were a sales flop and were only run once each as only the initial orders were ever received from the US importer, so they are not common models today. March 1965 saw the launch of Corgi's first television tie-in model, #258 Volvo P1800 from *The Saint*, which was simply a white issue of the #228 Volvo P1800 with a 'Saint' logo decal applied to the bonnet. It was a sales success, selling well over one million examples in its five years of production. Mettoy's out-of-the-box idea to modify the new #447 Ford ice cream van with Swiss-made five-note musical chimes and sell it as #474 was not a success and not repeated even though this writer's parents chose one as my first Corgi for my third birthday!

Fifty years on, of all the Corgi trucks made in the UK it is this Ecurie Ecosse racing transporter that still commands high prices yet sells easily, especially in this less common light metallic blue. (Vectis)

This gold plated #261 Aston Martin has been with the family of Corgi director Henry Ullmann since new – sadly the plating hasn't stood the test of time and finger grease! It failed to reach its reserve of £2,400 when offered for sale by Vectis in 2018.

Just in time for the Christmas shopping season in October, Corgi released the earliest production of the James Bond *Goldfinger* Aston Martin DB5. Marcel Van Cleemput wrote that Howard Fairbairn had rejected the proposal to model the car when the film was released in September 1964; however, early in 1965 a change of heart resulted in a crash program to modify the existing #218 Aston Martin DB4 with a new DB5 front and superbly engineered movie gimmicks – ejector seat, sprung guns and rear shield – to get the #261 James Bond Aston Martin DB5 in stores as the most wanted toy for Christmas 1965. Most children were unaware that Corgi's colourful choice of gold paint for the *Goldfinger* film car was inaccurate because only cinema goers over fourteen years of age were able to see the film in cinemas from 1964 to 1966, even though this toy made the younger ones want to see the film! The year ended with the first incarnation of the #256 VW Beetle with steering beginning its twelve years in the Corgi range fitted with rubber tyres, which it kept until 1977 as the last casting so fitted: the #401 Driving School VW.

Mettoy built up Corgi sales and market shares in 1966, primarily with more film and TV cars, beginning with *The Avengers* gift set #40, using extant tooling for the #9002 Bentley and #318 Lotus Elan. The #497 *Man from U.N.C.L.E* (TV show) car was represented by the old #235 Oldsmobile Super 88 fitted with figures and a steel spring mechanism that produced gunfire sounds when the roof periscope was depressed rather than any cars actually used on the show. Howard Fairburn is credited by Marcel Van Cleemput for obtaining the rights

Marcel Van Cleemput really captured the essence of the #485 Austin Mini Countyman and the #448 and #450 Mini van with these three models, which are very collectable today, especially among owners of full-size Minis.

to make the #267 Batmobile while at the 1966 New York toy fair, just after *Batman* had debuted on US networks. It was Corgi's second most iconic toy and hit stores just in time for the Christmas shopping season in October 1966. The first run was painted in the satin black finish of the actual TV car in the earliest press photos, but subsequent runs were in the glossy black familiar from actual episodes. Marcel Van Cleemput owned Mettoy's engineering prototype for a proposed steering model of *Thunderbirds'* FAB 1 Rolls-Royce; however, overconfident Corgi lost out to their main rivals when Dinky Toys licensed the exclusive rights to make superb toys of Gerry Anderson's *Thunderbirds* and all subsequent series – *Captain Scarlet, Joe 90, UFO* and *Space: 1999*.

1967 was the year Corgi's sales peaked at almost 17.5 million full-sized Corgis, eleven years after the brand launched and eight years after Dinky Toys' sales peaked way back in 1959. Corgi continued doing what it did best with the James Bond Toyota 2000GT, the year's best new film model. The Green Hornet's Chrysler *Black Beauty* was the year's best new TV model, featuring a flying radar scanner and concealed firing missile – a superb toy that sold around a million pieces even though the TV series was a flop never shown in the UK. 1967's most out-of-the-box gimmicks were on the #262 Lincoln Continental stretch limo, which featured flock textured interior and a built-in TV set which offered kids a choice of two photos to insert, all packed in a bubble on a blistercard rather than a box, marking a new direction in packaging.

1968 was the year Corgi raised the quality design bar even higher for the industry with their best ever detailed new toys. Corgi finally made a proper 1/43 scale James Bond Aston Martin DB5, which was released as #270 in February in authentic silver to replace the gold 1/45 #261 version, which had sold almost 4 million units in the previous twenty-eight months,

This factory colour trial Porsche Carrera 6 shows a colour considered but rejected by Corgi; note also the lack of blue tint in the rear screen. It survived with the family of director Henry Ullmann to be auctioned by Vectis in 2018 for £800 plus buyer's premium.

These are the four variations of the Porsche Carrera 6 that were actually sold in large numbers, the vast majority being race #60 with red trim. Only one run of navy blue trimmed examples were made and race #1 was a gift set only model.

just about wearing out the tooling. With added tyre slashers and revolving numberplates, this superb model was in production until 1978, latterly modified for tooling wear and fitment of Whizzwheels! Many kids' favourite gimmick, the 'Golden Jacks' take off wheels were initially fitted to two existing castings (#252 and #264) reissued as the #275 Rover 2000TC and the #276 Oldsmobile Toronado, with two more new for 1968 castings as well: the #338 Camaro and #341 Mini Marcos. A strong contender for the best model Corgi ever made was the #335 Jaguar E Type released in June 1968 with opening door, bonnet and tailgate, tilting and sliding seats, cast wire wheels, cast exhaust and chromed bumpers – a true adult collectable as well as an excellent toy. Corgi dazzled the Christmas shopping season with their iconic #266 *Chitty Chitty Bang Bang* from the movie of the same name, with intricate details – including a return to 1950s tinplate stamping for the hood – never matched on mainstream toy cars since. It was packaged in the new standard window box looking as if flying through a cloud – a magical Christmas or birthday gift for kids who had seen the movie, priced at 22*s* 6*d* in an era when the average child was given between 6*d* and 1s pocket money each week.

Two low budget new models (from old tooling) which were not in keeping with Corgi's expanding brand values for 1968 were the #348 Pop Art Mustang and the #349 Pop Art Mini, both decorated with Flower Power style decals. They didn't appear in any catalogues and the #348 Mustang was only on order forms for six months and sold poorly. Only a few gross of the #349 Mini were shipped to Denmark and distributed to high end toy stores there as a collectable beween late 1968 and early 1969. This #349 Mostest Mini and the un-numbered all yellow Coleman's Mustard promo version of the same car both sell for £500 or more when they turn up in near mint condition. Remaining stocks of both models were destroyed alongside the total contents of the factory warehouse in a fire

The Golden Jacks #275 Rover 2000TC was a big seller in metallic green with brown seats – modelled on a one-off motor show car for the USA with a triplex glass roof. However, there was one hard-to-find short run in white with maroon seats, as well as models using leftover maroon seats and white seats being used up in the production of otherwise standard metallic green Rovers. (Vectis)

The Ford H series truck was a superbly engineered toy with a lot of delicate parts, making it costly to manufacture, so it was used with the car transporter as well as other loads. Corgi included special colour models with these gift sets to make sure kids didn't just get cars in the same colours they already had. Specials included this metallic wine red Rover which was the old Trans-o-lite #252 model with hard ivory plastic seats from the Golden Jacks #275. Also, the bronze #251 Imp, both with and without white side flash, and the grey Ford Cortina woody estate were recolours just for #GS41. (Vectis)

The Mettoy factory and warehouse fire of 10 March 1969 destroyed all stocks held by the company in Swansea on that day – among the burnt models subsequently recovered from a Midlands smelter as recently as 2010 were the smoky, oxidised remains of at least a dozen blue Husky Cadillac Eldorados from the base of a slagheap against a wall. Large quantities of other damaged models and figures were recovered in the late 1980s and early 1990s from the cleared Swansea factory site from where they had been bulldozed after the fire. Part of *The Great Book of Corgi 1956–1983* by Marcel Van Cleemput is visible in this photo.

on Monday 10 March 1969. The warehouse was at that time grossly overstocked, in part due to the unanticipated decline in sales of big Corgis in 1968 by 3 million compared to 1967 as well as the massive fall in exports to the USA of Husky, which Woolworths were finding hard to sell to kids who wanted Hotwheels! Mettoy thus spent 1969 building stocks of models for the coming Christmas market in particular from a zero base in a different warehouse.

Corgi's new model release program was unaffected by the loss of the warehouse stock, with the most remarakable odd choice for a new model being the #803 cartoon Yellow

Submarine from The Beatles movie of the same title. Most controversial was the #801 Enid Blyton's Noddy car featuring friend Golly in the back seat for the initial production run, but replaced by Mr Tubby for subsequent production. September 1969 saw the release of the very first Red Spot Whizzwheels model – the #344 Ferrari Dino – followed a month later by the #347 Chevy Astro. It is important for collectors to be aware that Corgi only ever released five models from the factory with Red Spot wheels, the #343 Pontiac Firebird and #303 and #311 Ford Capris being the other models. Anything else sold today on eBay is a simple wheel swap from one of these five.

Did You Know?

Marcel Van Cleemput obtained permission from motor manufacturers and branded product rights owners before any model could become a Corgi. Corgi rarely cast or applied makers' badges to toys; however the #271 Ghia DeTomaso Mangusta, which was modelled after a visit to the factory in Italy, faithfully reproduced the Ghia logo on the bonnet and baseplate of the toy. When Ghia, a separate company from De Tomaso, saw their logo on the first run Corgi #271, they contacted Corgi, insisting that their name and logo be removed from all Corgi cars and boxes. Thus all subsequent runs of the #271 and #203 are named the De Tomaso Mangusta and have a fictional logo on the bonnet and a blank on the base. Corgi Juniors #6 is also simply just named De Tomaso Mangusta. The orange skirt version shown on the box art was never sold in shops, perhaps as a result of the fire destroying stocks.

The last two Golden Jacks models were released early in 1970 – the #273 Rolls-Royce and the #300 Corvette – before the factory went full speed into Whizzwheels conversions of exisitng models. Other new model cars released reflected the move towards Whizzwheels and bright colours, although trucks and farm vehicles remained as realistic as possible but simpler in design and with fewer parts than their 1960s counterparts.

In October 1970 Corgi delivered thousands of their new #313 Ford Cortina GXL to the Ford Motor Company to be used for the official launch of the full-size Cortina Mark 3. It was in a caramel colour with black vinyl roof that was a close approximation to the actual maize yellow two-door GXL model used by Ford in most UK launch advertising. A month later, Corgi sent out stocks of the new #313 Cortina in their own choice of colours, metallic light

Another Corgi gift set car transporter featuring a cost-saving sticker to update an obsolete box as well as some special coloured cars not realised in individual boxes. Note the orange MGC GT, all or most of which revealed yellow paint from surplus #345 bodies under the orange. Later rare Whizzwheels versions contained a blue #341 Mini Marcos, a pearl white #377 Marcos and the unsold remains of the candy purple #281 Rover 2000TC production. (Vectis)

blue and metallic dark copper, which were brighter approximations of Ford colours, boxed up with a figure representing F1 World Champion Graham Hill, who did some promotional appearances for Ford at that time. All #313 Cortinas had guidelines cast into the bodywork for mask spraying dayglow police stripes, although due to production priorities the big selling #402 Police Cortina didn't make it into the shops before August 1972.

Corgi also delivered about a thousand #306 Morris Marinas to British Leyland for the 27 April 1971 launch of the Morris Marina – the Corgis being given away to invited guests, employees and dealership sales reps. The management of huge rivals Ford and British Leyland thus had total confidence in Corgi's ability to model their newest cars in total secrecy, in synch with the launch dates of the real new cars.

Cult film *A Clockwork Orange* featured the obscure Adams Probe 15, which Corgi released in December 1970, a whole year before the film premiered in cinemas, although Corgi's decision to make it and the film prop casting both date to the summer of 1970, so they could be related.

The #273 Golden Jacks Rolls-Royce was the author's favourite childhood Corgi – his tenth birthday gift – a superb model with maximum opening features. This is the rarer of the two-tone colours used for this model before it was cheapened but made to roll faster with Whizzwheels. (Vectis)

Mettoy reported their first ever annual trading loss (£441,000) in their accounts for 1970 as toy car sales continued to fall, resulting in the 1971 closure of the second factory unit in Northampton as well as the firing of 900 employees, half the Northampton workforce. As a consequence Mettoy increased efforts to expand the non-diecast side of their business, starting with a five-year contract to manufacture Fisher Price toys. This reflected intensifying competition in a shrinking world diecast market with a

Special order colour and mask sprayed stripe made for the Ford Motor Company launch of the Ford Cortina Mark 3 in October 1970. Ford despatched most of their launch #313 Cortina Mark 3 order to their European dealerships that would sell new Cortinas, which included Denmark, Sweden, Norway and Holland. Note the Nordic box label – very rare!

A very rare colour issue – a special order with Blaze orange paintwork and black interiors made for British Leyland to give away at the Cowley factory launch of the Morris Marina, which gave prominence to Blaze and pinkish beige (Bedouin) coloured Marina Coupés.

new trend beginning for children to lose interest in toy cars at a younger age while robust diecast toys were passed on, capable of outlasting multiple childhoods. Sadly, Mr Phillipp Ullmann, the company President and founder, died in 1971 – thus he wasn't witness to the decline and breakup of all that he had built, or the revival of the Corgi name, heritage and stature that Marcel Van Cleemput contributed to in his retirement over twenty years.

Did You Know?

To help promote Whizzwheels as an innovation in 1971 and 1972, Corgi featured box art and advertising with cartoon characters called 'The Corgi Technocrats' – a brave but comical marketing attempt to boost sales which Marcel Van Cleemput regarded as cringeworthy and not resembling any specific Mettoy employees, least of all himself!

1971 was the year in which Marcel Van Cleemput designed a superb group of models inspired by dragsters that he had seen on the world class Santa Pod raceway near the Northampton factory – they looked as fast as they rolled, although the 1/43 size track sets that Corgi began to manufacture on which to race them and other big Whizzwheels cars were only made in small numbers before being withdrawn from production not long after the 1972 collectors catalogue had been printed in January of that year. When Corgi lost the Tracksets patent court case brought by Mattel, Marcel Van Cleemput wrote that the tooling for the track sets was dumped into Swansea harbour. These dragsters introduced an innovation – Whizzwheels tyres with hollowed out centres, fitted with

Here are Corgi's 1/43 scale Ford Capri issues – the sales of this model likely contributed to the huge popularity of the Ford Capri Mark I which has given it iconic classic status beyond the generation who bought them new!

chrome-plated moulded rims or hubcaps in different alloy styles. This improvement made plain Whizzwheels much more attractive and less of a step down from rubber tyres, although these better quality wheels were only fitted to the more expensive models. June 1971 saw these wheels used on Corgi's penultimate 1/43 car, tooled with full detailing with wire suspension, opening doors, tailgate and tilting seats – the superb #284 Citroën SM, which was only spoiled by the blue interior clashing badly with its pearl pink or pearl lime paintwork.

Late in 1971 Corgi obtained a license to manufacture figures and items from the five-minute children's puppet TV show *The Magic Roundabout*, which had a cult following among under-sixes. However, this proved to be a major financial error of judgement because such small children were too young to appreciate the extremely costly, highly detailed *Magic Roundabout* sets although they are very collectable today. A *Basil Brush* car #808 with a cheesy laugh sound box and a *Hardy Boys* cartoon Flower Power #805 Rolls-Royce were also sales flops, targeted at kids who didn't regard cars as being fun or key parts of enjoying those shows if, that is, they watched them at all! But collectable today...

January 1972 saw the launch of the #393 Mercedes 350SL, Corgi's final 1/43 scale, highly detailed car with multiple opening parts – a sales success produced into 1979. 1972 also saw the release of two James Bond models, the #391 Mustang and #811 Moon Buggy from the film *Diamonds are Forever*, which were both sales disappointments; only one production run of each was done until the original Mustang tooling was revived in the late 1990s in China to reissue it alongside the James Bond Toyota 2000GT #336 from *You Only Live Twice*.

The sole Golden Jacks model never converted to Whizzwheels, the Hillman Hunter GLS rally car, exists only in protype Whizzwheels form representing Chrysler dealerships' 1972 Castrol saloon car championship racers FWK700L/FWK800L. Vectis auctions sold this prototype from the Marcel Van Cleemput collection that he kept long after he had sold the vast bulk of his collection off after finishing *The Great Book of Corgi* – I suspect he regretted that this model was never approved for production.

Exclusive Netherlands-only Rijkspolitie liveries for the #509 Porsche 911 are hard to find but surprisingly accurate when compared to museum exhibits today. The German Polizei issue was exported worldwide in large numbers but dot pattern wheels were pre-1973 only.

3

Husky – The Pocket Money Toys

A 1964 pre-production Husky Mercedes 200S in candy dark red with very light grey wheels as sold by Vectis for £620 + fees for the family of Corgi director Henry Ullmann (son of the Mettoy founder). This 1/72 scale toy was only ever sold in pale blue.

The Husky brand was created by Mettoy to rival Lesney's Matchbox 1-75 series for the Woolworths chain of stores that were a common sight on the high streets of the UK and main streets of North America in the 1960s and 1970s. The first choice name, 'Husky Toys', was used for mock-ups and sample blisterpacks made for the approval of Woolworths in the US; however, the discovery that a Canadian tinplate truck maker had already trademarked the name Husky Toys resulted in the range being branded and launched as 'Husky Models'. Many children and adults over the years have referred to Husky Models from the makers of Corgi Toys as Husky Toys, which is an entirely logical mistake to make, especially when those trademarked Canadian tinplate Husky Toy trucks were never as well known to children or adult collectors as Mettoy's Huskys.

The initial fifteen Husky Models were available from all Woolworths stores in good time for the Christmas 1964 shopping season. Husky Models were also distributed via normal Corgi distribution chains in many countries which did not have Woolworths stores. In the same way that Corgi gained an edge over Dinky, the plan for Husky was to offer better quality 3-inch scaled cars at the same Matchbox price point. Husky's unique selling points

This group of Husky models was sold by Vectis for director Henry Ullmann's family and fetched £580 plus commission. Note the Ferrari in candy dark red with yellow seats, the same as the Hong Kong-made Mini Dinky issue, the colour trial 64 mm Citroen Safari – metallic blue was only used on the 70 mm post-1966 version – and the James Bond Aston Martin DB6 lacking blue tinted glazing. Also, the pink Thunderbird still has its easily lost black tonneau.

Here are the three variations of the Husky Sunbeam Alpine – for reasons unknown, Corgi failed to tie this model to Mel Brooks' cult TV show *Get Smart*, which would have required black seats to go with the candy red paint.

were sprung suspension and chrome-plated bumpers/baseplates as well as Woolworths' favoured clear bubble blisterpack on corporate coloured red and white backing cards, which naturally needed no store display cases, just standard pegs.

Pre-production examples still exist of most of the first fifteen models, fitted with blank baseplates manufactured prior to the Husky brand name being signed off as a logo without any embellishment, without the word 'Models' (or 'Toys') on the plastic baseplates. Small quantities of early Husky Models catalog numbers 1–15 were made with champagne-tinted vaccuum-plated baseplates and are believed to have been sales samples – they are very sought after today. Unfortunately, the plastic formulation to create the sprung suspension required a hardness compromise that enabled sweaty hands or simply sunlight shining on a brand new blisterpacked Husky to cause the vaccuum-applied chrome plating to crumble or

Woolworths USA specified that prices should be printed on their Husky blistercards; otherwise, those for the rest of the world were identical 1964–69. Note the small flakes of chrome around the yellow car, which is still factory sealed; this shows that this specific car has been heated by sunshine, causing chrome to flake off the baseplate. The Commer Walkthru truck was a brilliant choice that was never exploited for advertising and promotions – prototypes exist with metal not plastic sliding doors.

flake off baseplates easily and the suspension was brittle enough to break in light play use or underfoot, unlike the robust Matchbox.

The original lineup of Husky Models were manufactured at the Swansea factory, looked good in bright colours and were scaled to be attractive to railway modellers as well as children, which made most of the initial fifteen models significantly smaller sized than typical 1964 Matchbox models. As with big Corgis, some models featured new innovations, which included removable plastic canopies/roofs. Sales were strong from the very beginning and the range was expanded via a new release every six weeks or so, reaching thirty-two models by Christmas 1966.

The first fifteen Husky Models illustrate how Mettoy was inspired by Lesney Matchbox toys. Most were very close to 1/72 scale; however, perhaps the first to be tooled up, the Lancia Flamina, was to the even smaller 1/76 railway modeller scale and a very odd choice for a range of toys aimed primarily at the US and secondly at the UK, where Lancia Flaminas were rarely if ever seen on the streets by children or anybody else! The Jaguar Mark X, Citroën Safari, Buick Electra and Guy Warrior tipper tooling supplied two models each while the Volkswagons used the same baseplate and glazing even if the body featured very different cargo areas. Thus Mettoy created a fifteen-model range using ten and a half sets of tooling. 1965 saw eight new Husky models added and 1966 saw ten more to their original formula.

1967 was the year Mettoy acted to resolve their 1964 design compromises by replacing most of the underscaled castings from the 1964 initial range with longer, wider Matchbox-scaled 'fill the box' size models as the competition heated up with Lesney. The new tooled models with chrome-plated plastic baseplates were put into production, expanding the range to thirty-six models as were the first truly sturdy Husky Models with the new standard diecast chemically plated or painted metal baseplates fitted with strong piano wire sprung suspension just as big Corgi Toys had. These new metal baseplate models carried full branding as 'Husky Models' rather than the previous 'Husky'.

1968 was the year that new Huskys gained wheels with diecast hubs or plated hubcaps on black tyres in place of the previously universal dark grey plastic wheels – a response to Lesney's 1967 innovation of fitting chrome-plated hubs to new model cars. The range grew to remain stable at a planned thirty-six models although there were now some gaps in the series as well as new models 38–40. The release of Mattel's new Hotwheels from 18 May 1968 made a huge dent in sales volumes in the US, but less of an impact in the UK and Europe when Hotwheels cost about 150 per cent of the retail price of a Husky or Matchbox toy. Mettoy's innovation for 1968 resulted in Husky Extras – higher priced, superbly detailed TV/film models inspired by full-sized Corgis – although the first issue, the #1001 James Bond Aston Martin DB6, was based upon modifying the new Husky #22 DB6 tooling with the addition of an ejector seat, rather than creating a correct Husky-sized Aston Martin DB5 toy. Mettoy's response to the

Big Corgi details at a pocket money price was the logic behind Husky Extras – this 1969-only yellow card shows Corgi's new Aston Martin DB6 casting (never used in any Bond movie) substitutes for the Goldfinger DB5, which was never a Husky or Juniors casting. (JP)

The Husky Extra Batboat was sold singly as well as in gift packs – this example has export model product code 1403 rather than UK code 1003. (JP)

Christmas 1968 sales results was to cut back the 1969 new Husky models program from twelve planned releases to four actual ones and divert those resources into creating the initial seven models of the new Corgi Rockets range.

Woolworths in the US cancelled their exclusive deal with Mettoy for 1969, reflecting the massive decline in sales of Husky Models as well as Matchbox Toys in the US in the second half of 1968 due to the success of Mattel's Hotwheels. Woolworths in the US also chose to commission a new range of exclusive low-friction wheeled cars from Playart of Hong Kong, in part because Mettoy was not prepared to supply their new planned faster than Hotwheels range at Woolworths' target price point, let alone offer exclusive rights to the new Corgi Rockets. Woolworths in the UK continued to stock now slow-selling Huskys with uninterrupted supplies flowing, but sold side by side in every high street with Matchbox Superfast models from the Christmas shopping season in 1969.

Mettoy responded to their new freedom to sell Husky models throughout North America and the UK by changing the Husky blister card design for 1969 from Woolworths' red and white to the Corgi yellow with white logo on a red block. Mettoy also took their traditional but, by 1969, very cheap looking solid grey plastic wheels out of production (except for the Batmobile with its special rear-axle-driven exhaust flame), upgrading all models that were current for 1969 that hadn't previously been specified with black-tyred wheels with either diecast hubs or plated hubs. It was planned to rebrand Husky Models as Corgi Juniors now that Mettoy had the freedom to link their 3-inch range to the big Corgi brand; however, that would have to wait until 1970 as for the rest of 1969 factory resources prioritised the October 1969 launching of 'Corgi Rockets' cars and track sets to compete head on with Hotwheels that Christmas season as well as getting the first 1/43 scale Whizzwheels into shops.

Above: Owners of full-sized Ford Transits collect both the Husky and Juniors versions. Here are all the colours and wheel patterns it was issued in – the extremely rare green Husky in the yellow blisterpack is believed to have come from Corgi at the 1969 Nuremberg toy fair.

Left: This Corgi Tourist car park carry case was made in both a Husky and a Corgi Junior version – interestingly, the parking bases are just about big enough to be used with big Corgis too so this was very well designed, although it is uncommon today. The superb models shown are 1969–70 late Huskys and early Corgi Juniors that were a sales flop in the USA when kids could have a Hotwheels or Matchbox Superfast for the same money.

4

Corgi Rockets and Juniors – with Whizzwheels

Did You Know?

Woolworths were Corgi's biggest customer in the UK from 1971 onwards. Woolworths sold the vast majority of the Corgi Juniors sold in the UK. Corgi packaged some exclusive items like the Corgi Rockets Wall of Death track set as well as offering much of its remaindered stocks cheaply for Woolworths to sell.

The solarbrite copper Rockets Mercedes 280SL is one of those rare colour variations first publicised by Ed Force in his books – this photo compares it to the silver version with the wheels Marcel Van Cleemput designed it to have as a Husky model in 1969. James Bond black and dayglo green issues are also rare compared to standard blue issues. Most of the production of these short runs was sold new in the USA.

From the May 1968 launch of Mattel's revolutionary Hotwheels it became obvious that, for the first time in the twelve years since the launch of the Corgi brand, Mettoy were no longer the toy car market's leading innovators and that their investment in Husky tooling was under severe threat with the collapse in Woolworths US sales, which had accounted for more than half of Husky production. Mettoy has never released any precise figures; however, they were likely a similar reduction in sales to Lesney, who claimed that their actual post-Hotwheels launch 1968 US sales of the 1-75 series declined to only 10 per cent (from previous levels of 60 per cent) of the 5 million cars produced each week in 1968. Both Mettoy and Lesney entered 1969 holding massive stocks of unsold models, although Mettoy's factory and warehouse fire of 10 March 1969 destroyed all of the company's stock in the warehouse. Hotwheels changed the previously established norms of toy car play overnight from realistic looking cars familiar from local streets to free wheeling, track racing and flashy candy coloured design concepts, California custom or fantasy cars. Mattel is likely even to have taken inspiration from Husky's chrome Jaguar Mark X and Lesneys #32 candy red Jaguar E-Type, which looked fast even when they were not! Mattel engineers used 1967 Matchbox models as engineering mules to design Hotwheels – not Huskys!

In the US from 1968 to 1970 Hotwheels cost 79–89 cents in stores and Lesney Matchbox 49–59 cents each, while Huskys were pitched 10 cents cheaper by Woolworths. For the rest of the world Hotwheels were a premium product, generally costing half as much again as a Matchbox 1-75 series. Mettoy's 1969 strategy was to create their own premium very

Champagne gold was never a standard Corgi Rockets colour although this extremely rare Jaguar XJ6 from the Simon Philips collection may have been an early 1970 Nuremberg and New York Trade toy fairs promotional exclusive. It is seen in a standard Rockets blisterpack.

This movie poster-inspired *On Her Majesty's Secret Service* James Bond blister design made such an impression on the author aged eight that he has treasured it ever since – it has survived the decades well considering it has been used a fair bit. This Ford Escort represents the car driven by Roger Clark in the movie – Corgi also modelled his 4WD Ford Capri.

fast cars with better candy colours and better track designs to capture a market share one Christmas season later than Mattel's launch. This was in stark contrast to Lesney Matchbox's winning strategy to keep their prices steady while offering Superfast rolling performance at approximately two thirds of the price of a Hotwheels or Corgi Rocket worldwide.

Mettoy launched their initial seven Corgi Rockets models and the first track sets in October 1969. The cars chosen were the sportiest new bodyshells intended for Husky models and the planned Corgi Juniors range. For both play value and track speed, a heavy diecast baseplate combined with a detatchable nylon chassis (which could be removed with a golden key plus clip-on axles) made from the same black plastic as the tyres gave Corgi Rockets comparable track performance to similar weighted Hotwheels. There was also the added advantage that the Rockets' thicker stainless wire axles didnt bend or buckle – a design weakness and compromise made by both Matchbox Superfast and Hotwheels to provide superb suspension that Corgi Rockets didn't need.

Corgi came up with costly 'Solarbrite' paint, a clear candy-tinted vaccuum metalised plating which gave a mirror finish that lasted – a quality shared by US-made Topper cars but not Hotwheels, which tended to tone within months, particularly if subjected to a lot of acidic hand sweat or if the casting had not been tumbled sufficiently before spectraflame paint was applied.

The mint green #24 Aston DBS from the Christopher Cousins collection on the right is very rare, tending to sell for around £200 mint on the blisterpack – it may well have been Corgi's 1971 Nuremberg and New York Trade toy fairs special.

Surviving factory colour trial cars show that Mettoy considered all the familiar solarbrite colours plus plain chrome and champagne gold (both never specified for retail Rockets) as well as dayglo safety colours for just about all of the Rockets castings before assigning one or two unique colours or shades to each model. To make the most of the expensive tooling, most castings appeared or were intended to appear as two different coloured Rockets models, in contrast to the Hotwheels colour strategy, which made each of their initial sixteen castings in a rainbow of at least seven different colours.

Did You Know?

The 1969 James Bond Film *On Her Majesty's Secret Service* was the third Bond film that Corgi decided to create toys for, but they chose to showcase the Bond cars in their new fast rolling Corgi Rockets range. Marcel Van Cleemput photographed and measured up GKX 8G, the 1969 Aston Martin DBS used in the film, as well as the red Mercury XR7 convertible it chased in the opening scene. Due to a dispute between the film's producers and its star actor, George Lazenby, who had refused to sign a new contract, Corgi were ordered not to release the planned #D929, but the metallic dark olive paint had already been delivered from suppliers. As a result, the planned #D937 Mercury XR7 used up this paint instead of appearing in lime, as shown in the catalogue. The Aston Martin DBS tooling appeared as blue Corgi Rocket #D913, and also as Corgi Junior #24 using the lime paint intended for #D937.

Some of the new Corgi Juniors models released in 1970 were specifically designed with Corgi Rockets chassis sized wheelbases even though their Rockets versions were cancelled during 1970 following acceptable track performances of the cheaper-to-make Whizzwheels versions and the start of legal action over patent infringement on track set

These two possibly unique surviving factory colour trial Corgi Rockets Volvo 1800S (only sold in white or red) show that Corgi experimented with every Rockets colour on each casting before making their individual choices, whereas from 1968 to 1972 Hotwheels made each car for sale in each of ten colours. Note the #937 Mercury XR7 in the centre painted with the metallic dark olive paint ordered for the cancelled #929 James Bond Aston Martin DBS.

designs by Mattel. The first three cancelled Rockets were not glamourous enough subjects at a time when Corgi was choosing exotics to model. The NSU RO80, VW Beetle, De Tomaso, Ogle Reliant Scimitar and Austin Healy Le Mans were all designed to accept standard Rockets chassis, so three of them would have been #D912/D914/D915. #D932, which was never released, is shown in catalogues as The Futura. D934/D935/D936/D938/D939/D940, also never released, were according to different sources likely to have been either the #32 Lotus Europa or #33 Jaguar E-type or #57 Caddy Hot Rod or #60 VW Double Trouble or recoloured issues of both the existing stockcars D919 and D920 with a Barry Lee version of the existing Ford Escort.

The massive Christmas 1969 success of Matchbox Superfast from their initial autumn 1969 launch at their price point of an average week's pocket money, against Corgi Rockets (and Hotwheels outside the USA) costing an average one and a half weeks' pocket money, would compel Mettoy in 1970 to rethink their strategy to re-focus on competing with Matchbox Superfast, not Hotwheels. Indeed, such was the success of Matchbox Superfast worldwide that they forced Mattel in 1971 to start cutting the costs of their loss-making Hotwheels to compete on price worldwide. From 1972 Mattel dropped costly candy paints in favour of traditional enamels as well as dropping suspension, nylon bushes and detailed redline wheels in favour of much lower cost axles and wheels clearly inspired by the welded Matchbox Superfast design.

In January 1971 Mettoy won the British Toy of the Year award for Corgi Rockets for their successes from the Christmases of 1969 to 1970 when the writing was already on the wall for the whole Rockets range, even though it included four newly released models from the James Bond film *On Her Majesty's Secret Service*. Two bobsleighs from the film were made as

Corgi Juniors rather than Rockets and it was the Juniors VW Beetle that was used with these in OHMSS gift set #3004. The OHMSS Corgi Rockets were sold together in gift set #978 and when they turn up today in the original boxes enclosing the blisterpacks, both #978 and #3004 fetch well over £1,000 each.

Once Corgi Juniors Whizzwheels models were in volume production with Corgi Rockets wide wheels and axles, it meant the end of the premium priced Corgi Rockets range in 1972. *Tom & Jerry* cars originally intended for the 1972 Tom & Jerry Rockets track set were always planned as Corgi Juniors with Whizzwheels while the final Rockets product, the Wall of Death track set made to sell in the run-up to Christmas 1972, contained a never made again white Corgi Juniors Capri and a 1/32 scale motorcycle (bought in from Britains Ltd) on a lame

This Corgi Juniors Extra James Bond *On Her Majesty's Secret Service* bobsleigh complemented the Corgi Rockets models released from the same film – an orange version represented the baddy played by Telly Savalas, who later became Kojak, also modelled by Corgi as a figure with his brown Buick!

The 1967 NSU RO 80 was a car ahead of its time – the company was taken over by the Volkswagen Audi group and this 1960s design looks a lot like Audis of the past twenty-five years. This toy is very rare and costly in blue enamel or white – note it wears a Whizzwheels conversion, proving that it was intended to fit Corgi Rockets chassis C to this casting if it had become a Rocket as planned in 1969. The Jensen Interceptor below shows the rushed simple Whizzwheels conversions given to many Corgi Juniors – thin steel axles combined with thin nylon wheels. This model is rare and costly in orange, very common in metallic wine and uncommon in metallic green.

Whizzwheels trolley that was left over from the production of big Corgi flop #681, which sold just 19,000 examples separately.

Corgi Juniors as a brand were launched early in 1970, initially pitched as big Corgi quality at pocket money prices. Many of the first Corgi Juniors were outwardly the same as the previous Husky models with the exception of the baseplate, which carried a paper 'Corgi Juniors' sticker applied to the blank area of the baseplate where the Husky name had been removed. During the tooling transition in preparation for the launch of Corgi Juniors in 1969, a significant quantity of yellow card Husky models were made with blank no-name baseplates. Thus, yellow #39 Jaguar XJ6 models can be found with Husky baseplates in red or yellow Husky blisters, with blank space unbranded baseplates also in yellow Husky biisterpacks or with a Corgi Juniors sticker applied to the blank area in a long card Corgi Juniors blisterpack without Whizzwheels branding.

The company did make every effort to recolour models as soon as stocks of painted Husky bodies were exhausted and as a result many very limited runs of certain colour

The two sizes of paper label that Corgi applied to the undersides of Husky models that joined the new Corgi Juniors series. Models without the Husky name or a sticker were likely made and sold in 1969 on that year's yellow blistercards.

variations were manufactured; these are very collectable today but, surprisingly, cost much less to buy on eBay than equally scarce Lesneys of 1969–70. For the US market launch Mettoy made a nationwide promotion offering free Corgi Juniors when car owners purchased enough petrol to qualify. Four models featured in the advertising: the #45 silver Mercedes 280SL; the #46 metallic maroon Jensen Interceptor; the #9 metallic green Cadillac Eldorado; and the #22 metallic green Aston Martin DB6, although some

Corgi Juniors' new blisterpacks featured a clever promotional cut-out collector card featuring artwork of the 1:1 toy modelled, which it was hoped would be a big hit with kids who had the 1960s habit of collecting and swapping factual picture tea or bubblegum 'trading' cards with a nicely printed book to glue the set in, one by one. These three show the evolution of the design, 1970–72.

other models may have been given away at some fuel stations. These were superb models, 3-inch versions of big Corgi quality with realistic looking wheels; however, sales results were very poor in the face of stiff competition from free rolling toy cars backed with advertising budgets from Hotwheels and Matchbox Superfast at the same pricepoint. This experience encouraged Mettoy to create Whizzwheels – almost as fast on tracks as Corgi Rockets but so much cheaper to make, enabling healthy profits to be earned at the Matchbox Superfast price point.

Did You Know?

Mettoy anticipated great success when they launched collector card series Corgi Juniors in the US, as shown by the factory-printed 55 cents price tag at a time when Matchbox Superfast were rising from 49 cents to 59 cents. However, as the second 25 cent red price tag shows, kids didn't want the same old slow Huskys in new-look packets, they wanted new Matchbox Superfast and even faster Hotwheels. So as a stopgap measure, almost all Corgi Juniors were speedily given Corgi Rockets axles with thin black nylon tyres that rolled almost half as fast as Matchbox Superfast. Mettoy's desperation to kick-start sales shows here as they printed red stickers describing new Whizzwheels as 'Super-Fast', which was as close as they could get to Superfast without infringing Lesney's trademark in the US.

Boxes for Corgi Juniors are very hard to find today. Thin Whizzwheels are illustrated on this accurate #45 Mercedes 280SL – the box was a failed Corgi experiment to copy the most widespread form of traditional packaging used by competitors Matchbox. Boxes did not increase sales in any noticeable way at a time when increasing proportions of Matchbox toys were sold from pegs in blisterpacks.

In the UK only Corgi Juniors Whizzwheels had a high profile nationwide launch, offering a free Whizzwheels Corgi Junior car when car owners purchased enough petrol to qualify; the yellow Mercedes 280SL with thin black Whizzwheels was used in the poster campaign at petrol stations and advertising elsewhere.

Advertised initially as 'Corgi Juniors with Whizzwheels', the cars themselves had 'Corgi Juniors Whizzwheels' on their baseplates once a model was actually fitted with Whizzwheels. Those castings which didn't have baseplates with sufficient wheelarch space to allow standard

Factory colour trial Corgi Juniors Extra #1007, TV's Ironside's Truck in the authentic silver grey seen on the show with working wheelchair lift. It was rejected as too drab so was only ever sold in blue (sold by Vectis for £460 + commission for the Ullmann family).

Above: Marcel Van Cleemput was rightly proud of the *Chitty Chitty Bang Bang* model, which was a design, engineering and quality control triumph – and perhaps the Corgi toy with the most appeal to adults! Arguably the most absurd conversion to Whizzwheels, the fragile *Chitty* wasnt a race winner on tracks but Mettoy still spent the money to do so, although it is rare today. It is seen with the Husky and big Corgi versions to compare.

Right: The Husky Extras Batmobile gained a retooled baseplate, giving it a Corgi Rockets ride height, with Juniors wheels, all in a special red Juniors blisterpack; however, this model was withdrawn in 1972 and was replaced a couple of years later by a super-cheap, much simpler casting with plastic baseplate.

Note the 'Tested By The Corgi Technocrats' artwork on Club racing gift set 3020. This set contained the unique dark blue Corgi Juniors trailer (in many sets towed by a very rare Capri in matching paint) which wasn't sold in any form other than as a Corgi Rocket in yellow in two stockcar sets.

Corgi distorted the Volkswagen Beetle when they created their second set of tooling to make certain that the car would be fast on Rockets track sets. Most were painted in shades of green; however, there were also gift set versions in metallic blue as well as the rare metallic turquoise illustrated. The hole in the roof for the police variation was usually covered by a flower sticker. (Christopher Cousins)

The last thin Whizzwheels models produced in 1972 were these rare red enamel Jaguar XJ6s, which were made as tow cars for gift sets and a two-pack with a boat and trailer at a time when almost nothing in the Juniors range except for the Fire Chief Capri and Land Rover pickup had a tow hook. Vectis sold these rare leftovers issued on single cards. Note that the car on the right has wide Whizzwheels clearly rubbing against the bodywork, made to turn obsolete parts into saleable product.

free rolling Corgi Rockets wheels to be fitted were deleted from the range in 1971–72 or, in a few cases, given new baseplate designs with Rockets wheels. Five of the higher priced Husky Extra film and TV models were also converted to Whizzwheels, making them fast rolling toys rather than previously superb Husky models!

Thin Whizzwheels models were phased out in 1973 with the final casting, the Jaguar XJ6, being used as a tow car in gift sets and multipacks. When the decison was taken in 1973 to drop the collector picture card blisterpacks, a generic swirl on a red, blue or orange background became the new standard package for the range and this heralded the long decline in quality of the whole Corgi Juniors range as all-plastic baseplates with traditional Husky sprung suspension became standard on new Whizzwheels models from the #15 Schoolbus, which trended away from previously favoured realistic street vehicles.

Mettoy included many film and TV related toys in the Juniors range for the last ten years of their existence with some, like the *Liberator* from BBC TV's *Blake's 7*, obscure but commercially successful choices. A new lightweight Batmobile plus Kojak's Buick and the *Starsky & Hutch* Ford Torino in particular were huge sellers, albeit crude by 1968 standards. These models are not so collectable today, being of inferior quality all round; however, those who had them as children tend to like collecting these cheaper toys, which were never again equal, let alone superior, to metal baseplate Matchbox Superfast models.

Corgi chose to model the facelifted version of the huge selling diesel Mercedes W115 240D in both 3-inch and 1/36 scale as it was an instantly recogniseable modern sedan sold worldwide that could be painted and decorated to fullfill all sorts of roles – these two factory colour trials sold by Vectis show typical Mettoy typed codes and were never seen in shops in these colours.

This Corgi Tourist case parking lot displays some of the best 3-inch releases from the late 1970s and early 1980s. Kojak's Buick, James Bond's convertible Range Rover, a selection of emergency vehicles and some of the big selling Mercedes 240D variations.

This Volvo 245 in purple with yellow-tinted glazing and interior is a very rare early production factory colour trial and sales sample model that belonged to the Danish importer of Corgi toys. This casting was made in a rainbow of colours, with bronze being hard to find.

Corgi released their Juniors Citroën Dyane over six years after Citroën launched the 1:1. Most were issued in yellow; however, this purple car with red interior was a sales sample supplied to the Corgi importer to Denmark. Metallic blue is also scarce today.

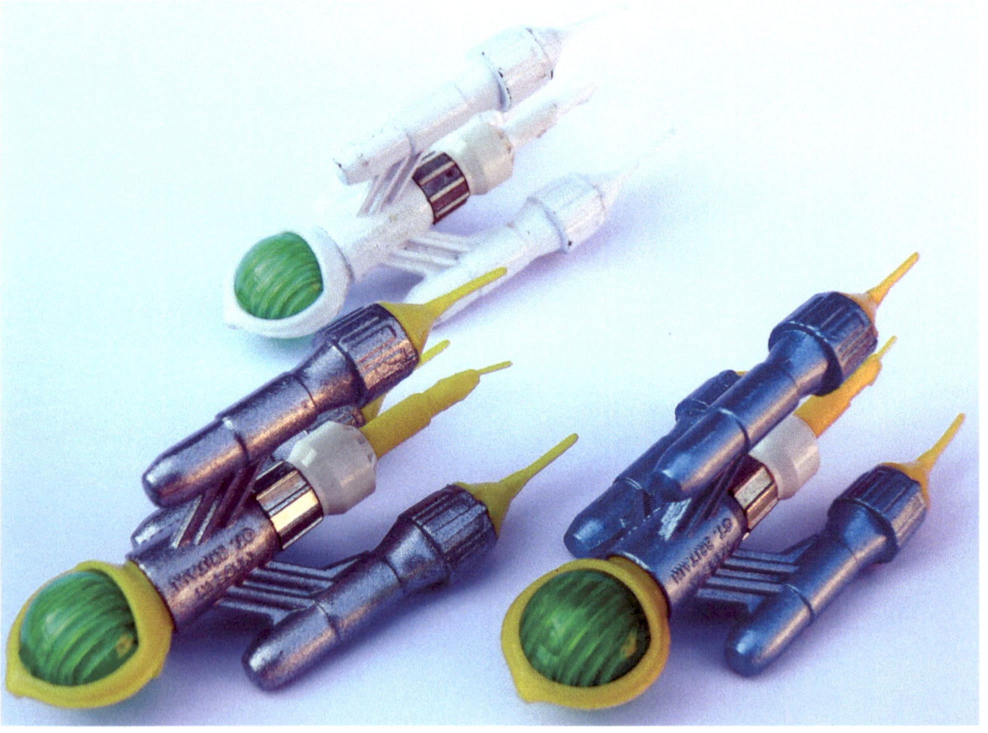

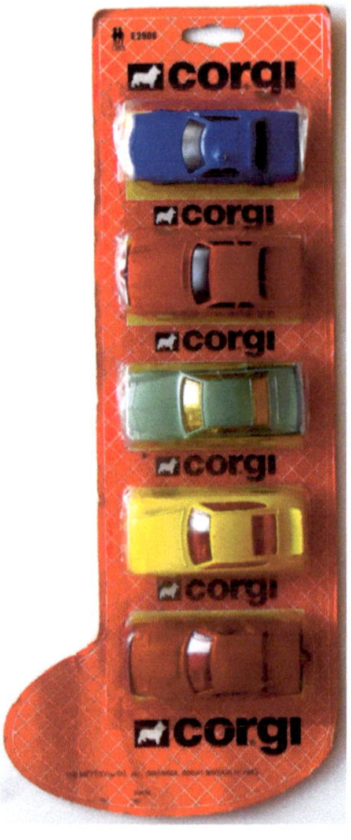

***Above**: Blake's 7* was BBC TV's ultra low budget serial response to the cinema's *Star Wars*. Corgi had a successful Juniors model of the Liberator, which is well known in silver or white but very rare in metallic blue. (Christopher Cousins collection)
Left: This Christmas stocking contained a random selection of 3-inch Corgis that had been painted with whichever colours were available when they were made between 1982 and 1983, with the blue *Starsky & Hutch* car and bronze TR7 being particularly uncommon.
Below: The Dodge Magnum only appeared in Corgi catalogues for 1980 and 1981. It was the most short-lived post-1973 3-inch Corgi, as well as the heaviest and most costly in terms of manufacturing, with its metal chromed base and opening bonnet.

Use of movie poster art on blistercards reflected the close two-way relationship between Mettoy and the producers of the James Bond franchise.

Use of colourful themed trade boxes like this Batman one from last days of Mettoy with Majorette-style inspired bubble boxes were a cost-cutting way of shipping and selling toys without the cost of having pegs or paying people to hang cards on them.

Instantly recognisable artwork and logos from popular current TV shows helped sell the toys, particularly as impulse buys, with a focus on shows that were popular in the UK, even if shows were made in America and many toys sold as export!

Corgi supplied its new 1/36 scale #299 Ford Sierra for the 1982 Ford UK launch of the Sierra as well as this 3-inch Corgi issue on a special Ford promo card to shops and dealerships. 'Juniors' had been dropped from the 3-inch range name in 1981.

5

Bigger Cars 1972–83

Did You Know?

Corgi often released new models on the same date as the full-sized cars, in agreement with the manufacturer; however, due to severe production delays at Jaguar, the Corgi #286 Jaguar XJC V12 was in toyshops from December 1974 but none from Jaguar reached showrooms or customers before the summer of 1975.

For 1972, Corgi made a commercial decision to create new car models in 1/36 scale, beginning with their new range of Formula 1 race cars which now looked more like a handful-sized car to a child than the almost Matchbox-sized 1960s Corgi F1 racers! The competitive edge from the greater visual impact on children of 1/36 over 1/43 more than justified the small percentage increases in materials, packaging and distribution costs. Corgi's market research showed the upper age limits for the vast majority of children getting new toy cars dropping

Yardley made 250,000 of these sets of soap plus the Formula I winner in their colours – their advance order made it easy for Corgi to prioritise this model. (Vectis)

below ten with no extra significant profits to be earned from teen or adult collector segments, who had dropped out of the 1/43 scale market with the advent of Whizzwheels and bright candy paints. With hindsight this appears to have been the correct way to go because main competitors Dinky adopted 1/36 scale in 1977 and 1/36 scale Corgis are very collectable today, particularly for those who had them new as children.

Rapid improvements in the standard of colour TV coverage of Formula 1 races gave Formula 1 cars, particularly the championship leaders' cars and sponsors, a high profile in the eyes of race fans of all ages. This was before the days of exclusive merchandise licenses being awarded by third parties with the approval of the administrators of the sport. The first model released was the Surtees TS9 in June 1972, which sold almost a half million examples by the end of 1974. Marcel Van Cleemput has written crediting John Surtees for helping Corgi with introductions to negotiate successfully with the other leading Formula 1 race car constructors to complete the company's Formula 1 range. These new models, in particular that 2 million seller introduced in March 1973, the #154 John Player Special Lotus in black trimmed with gold, helped Mettoy to report their best profit since 1968 as well as the only increase in diecast unit sales since 1968, although this was an exceptional result to interrupt the diecast sales contraction trend while remaining increasingly profitable for a few more years. Corgi sponsered a 1973 Le Mans entry, a Ferrari 365 Daytona which ran as car #33 and which was modelled faithfully by Corgi as #324, being released in June. This was in contrast to Lesney putting their Matchbox brand on a Formula 2 Surtees car for the season back in 1972 – a car, unsurprisingly, not modelled by Corgi!

Corgi found it profitable to add small scale diecast aircraft (most being 3 to 4 inches long), including the Concorde, to their range as well as superbly detailed tanks which rolled on rubber tracks in circa 1/60 scale, made to Corgi's specifications by Lin of Hong Kong for six years. No further production would be transferred to Asia under Mettoy's management of Corgi – interestingly, competitors Dinky dropped their Hong Kong production (Mini Dinkys and four American cars) after just a couple of years in 1969, although they resumed it in 1979 during the final efforts to save Dinky from bankruptcy.

Corgi continued to make and update both farm models and fire trucks, including Corgi's biggest single casting, the magnificent 1974 #1103 Chubb Pathfinder Airport Fire truck with working hose that could be loaded with water and squirted using a bladder. The other big casting in the range was the #190 1/18 scale F1 JPS Lotus, which sold well enough, but aside from the #191 F1 Marlborough McLaren, no further models in such a large scale were made.

In April 1975 Corgi issued #469, a new London Transport Routemaster casting in 1/65 scale which represented a standard bus and was a bit bigger and lighter and brighter coloured than the 1964 #468, modelled on a prototype. The 1975 production of this model featured driver and conductor figures which were deleted from the toy after the first run. This was to become a huge seller in hundreds of livery and label variations, with the tooling going to China and remaining in production well into the 1990s. 1975 was the year that Howard Fairbairn retired and Corgi's UK diecast unit sales fell below 1959 levels, although Mettoy increased profits.

1976 saw the legendary Mini 1000 re-issued in 1/36 scale (the tooling was still in production in China in 2018) with the retirement of the 1967 casting, latterly only used in 1975 as the #308 yellow Whizzwheels Monte Carlo winner and the London gift set. The same year, the 1/36 scale Land Rover Safari casting displaced the 1960s tool for the 1/43 #438 Land Rover 109 WB (although this tooling also went back into production in China this millenium).

Comparison between the bigger post-1975 #469 Routemaster with (rare) and without driver and the 1964–75 #468 prototype Routemaster.

ITV in the UK had the beginnings of a few years of ratings success transmitting the original *Batman* TV show from 1966–68 repeatedly, resulting in Corgi refreshing their Batmobile giftset #GS40 with the addition of a Batcopter – a substantial sales success and easily Corgi's best selling franchised themed gift set (when adding in almost ten years of selling Batmobile with Batboat #GS3), selling over 1 million 1/43 scale old tooling diecast Batmobiles in 1976 alone.

TV's *Kojak* featured a metallic brown Buick which Corgi brightened with copper metallic paint and sold in very large numbers, both in 1/36 scale as #290 and 1/64 Juniors scale from 1976, after the show had established itself in the UK. The white striped Ford Torino from TV's *Starsky & Hutch*, produced in 1/36 scale, followed in 1977 as #292 – yet another huge sales success, selling almost 1 million units over four years.

The best seller of 1977 was undoubtably the submarine Lotus Esprit that shoots mines from James Bond film *The Spy Who Loved Me*. 1977 was the year of HM Queen Elizabeth's Silver Jubilee and Corgi made a superbly detailed model of her 1902 State Landau hauled by four horses that reminds some toy collectors of the Coronation Coach that launched Matchbox into the world of wheeled diecast in 1953. Silver Jubilee issues of the London Routemaster bus sold very well and include very sought after small quantities of special versions featuring advertising from many of the companies who sponsered the twenty-five full-sized examples in London. But only Woolworths sold their Silver Jubilee Routemaster bus retail, as #471. Thus Mettoy was selling fewer diecast models but earning more profits thanks to fewer bigger selling film, TV and Formula 1 models as well as profitable non-diecast products.

The evergreen James Bond Aston Martin DB5 from the film *Goldfinger* was still selling well after twelve years in the range so Corgi refreshed it by investing in 1/36 scale re-tooling as #270 to make it the same scale as most of the other cars still in the range from May 1978. This left just the #280 Rolls-Royce, #384 VW Beetle, #393 Mercedes 350SL and #402 Police Cortina GXL (with a Range Rover and the Land Rover from gift set 109) as the final 1/43 scale vehicles left in the range six years after the switch to 1/36 scale. Corgi tried releasing a new circus gift set based upon Jean Richard's Circus; however it only sold 61,000 sets, failing to capture the imagination of 1970s children in the same way that Corgi's 1960s

Specially boxed Routemaster buses – the 1977 #471 Jubilee and 1977 Selfridges #467 were two of the three exceptions to Corgi's policy of issuing all Routemasters as #469 (from 1975 onwards) or as #468 (1964–75) in standard boxes.

Chipperfields toys had brought the previous generation of boys and girls together to play. Premuim customers for over twenty-five years, Marks & Spencers commissioned a range of St Michael branded gift sets in exclusive colours and liveries using existing tooling but with the Corgi name blanked out from baseplates – very collectable today, but rare boxed. The #320 Jaguar XJS for the re-booted *The Saint* TV series was the other notable new 1/36 scale tooling for the year.

1978 saw an increase in sales of almost three quarters of a million diecast toys – Corgi's last large increase in diecast sales and the Mettoy group's most profitable year ever. However, from 1979 rising costs made trading more difficult, although the group still made a small profit for the year. High interest rates on Mettoy's loans and a stronger sterling hitting export competitiveness really started to bite in 1980, with the company making its only trading loss since 1971 on falling sales. This worryingly huge £3.5 million loss was not Corgi-related, unlike in 1971 – it was other non-Corgi products like the Dragon computers under develpment combined with very high loan interest rates. Original main competitior Dinky Toys closed their Liverpool factory in November 1979, with plans to carry on production in Hong Kong under the same ownership dropped in the face of substandard toys and insufficient orders.

All kids know Superman doesn't require vehicles. However, for 1979 Corgi decided to try and cash in by issuing Corgis both big and small that were clearly identified with the franchise, with some sales success. *Moonraker* was the latest addition to the James Bond film franchise, with Corgi making the #649 Moonraker Shuttle, based on the NASA Shuttle, as well as using existing tooling to create other toys with links to the film which were launched at the London Odeon Leicester Square press preview of *Moonraker* – a sign that movie makers as well as motor manufacturers were happy to trust Corgi with advance images of vehicles before their public debut in order to have the toys on hand for the launches. The other big movie of 1979 that premiered with four new cartoon-style Corgi Toys (#2030–2033) in hand was the *The Muppet Movie*. These were designed by Marcel Van Cleemput but manufacture was subcontracted out to Hong Kong, continuing in the tradition of 1970s tanks, planes and plastic figures.

New models for 1980 included the latest incarnation of the Ford Capri as #342, tied to TV show *The Professionals*, #343 the street car and #312 the trackracer – a mere five years after Ford introduced the second body design! Corgi wasn't making toys for the *Star Wars* franchise; however, the next best thing in 1980 was TV's *Buck Rogers in the 25th Century* with new #647 being a well made Starfighter that fired missiles and came with figures of the two stars.

Solid demand in otherwise difficult trading conditions from importers in Germany, France and the Nordic countries for Corgi emergency services toys, big and small, in local liveries became a significant source of sales in 1979 that resulted in a new tool in 1980 to satisfy their demands for a vehicle unknown on UK roads: the #406/#407 Mercedes Bonna Ambulance. Corgi gave a unique product number, #333, to the special order new cast Ford Escort Mark 3 supplied directly to the Ford Motor Company for the European launch of the new Escort in 1980; the standard Corgi was #334. British Leyland launched the Austin Mini Metro on 8 October 1980, supported by a specially boxed new casting (#251) made as usual in total secrecy without press leaks. The Metro was also made as a Junior, and sold extremely well in both scales in all colours made, except the purple Royal issue reflecting Lady Diana's personal car before she married in 1981.

A late production example of the largest Batman gift set, now including helicopter, sold by Vectis.

Corgi used a lot of plastic making this Tarzan gift set, which is one of the most sought after 1/36 scale giftsets alongside the low volume Marks & Spencers specials, sold by Vectis.

The new James Bond film for 1981 was *For Your Eyes Only* and Corgi prepared a plain yellow Citroën 2CV 1/36 #272 in a special box for the film premier. The French motoring icon had never previously been made by Corgi although its out of production successor, the Citroën Dyane, was still in the current Corgi range! Corgitronics (#1002–1005) were the brand's final technical innovation – battery-powered, two-tone horns which could be activated by pressing down on the rear suspension. This gimmick more than doubled the selling price yet outwardly these looked like ordinary Corgis with blacked out windows, so it was no surprise that they weren't particularly profitable. Corgi supplied models of the #276 Triumph Acclaim for British Leyland's launch of their first Honda partnership product, also in 1981. The Ford Motor Company ordered thousands of new #299 Ford Sierras in their own design of box in time for the 13 October 1982 launch of the real Ford Sierra while Corgi had great success selling both big and small Corgi versions right to the end.The only new TV casting for 1982 was the #298 *Magnum, P.I.* Ferrari 308 GTS. Another new direction for 1982 was the Classics series of cars from the 1950s, based upon iconic designs like the gullwing Mercedes 300 SL (#802) – they were a profitable success, unlike the 1960s-made Classics series of veteran cars.

Corgi invested £115,000 in TV advertising in the post-Christmas 1981 to New Year 1982 period, hoping to earn kids' Christmas gift cash. However, Mettoy reported another big loss for 1981 that was only £700,000 less than the huge loss for 1980, even when combined with a £2 million improvement in sales over 1980. Clearly Mettoy was in deep trouble that was about to get worse, with high interest rates on loans in inflationary times and with investments in development of Dragon computers eating money but not yet paying off; however, diecast Corgis were still profitable. After taking into account more reductions in the workforce (by now less than one third of the 4,500 employed at the company's height), the 1982 results showed a massive £4 million loss on lower sales. As a result it was intended to close the Northampton facilities, with all remaining Mettoy activities, which were to be just administration, Corgi toys and Wembley balls, relocated to Swansea in 1983 although Mettoy went into receivership at the end of October 1983. Design work was contracted out to Marcel Van Cleemput, who ceased to be directly employed by Mettoy in 1983. His one notable new 1983 design, the last new Mettoy big Corgi, was the #1009 MG Maestro, supplied in quantity to British Leyland for their 2 March 1983 launch. It was a very basic 1/36 casting with no opening parts and no interior but did have blacked out windows to conceal batteries for the working front and rear lights – an uncommon model to try and find today.

Did You Know?

While all big Corgi toys were made in Wales, the earlier stages of the production process and administration were carried out in Northampton. Financial restructuring in 1982 to try and save Mettoy involved closing the original Northampton premises completely, with all remaining administration, production, design and engineering relocating to the spacious Swansea factory. However, as Marcel Van Cleemput wrote in his book, almost nobody was prepared to move to Wales so the irreplaceable engineering and toolmaking employees stayed on in Northampton while the rest left the company. The design department ceased to exist with Marcel, freelancing from home, covering all Mettoy's 1983 design requirements.

A Vectis auction lot showing four 1983 Mettoy-made Classics alongside three skidmark Corgi company collectables made in the late 1980s – the items are all common and inexpensive.

Early in 1984 there was a management buyout of the Corgi brand, with all tooling and machinery included, that became 'The Corgi Toy Company Limited', using the well known 'skidmark' logo and making a somewhat shoddy selection of the most recent Mettoy created Juniors and 1/36 scale models. All production moved to China in 1989, along with all diecast tools – all the 3-inch Juniors toolings ended their production life with Mattel between 1989 and 2003 while many big Corgi model tools remained with the post-Mattel independent, British-owned Corgi brand established in 1995 and went back into production, making adult collectables designed in the UK but made in China.

This lot sold by Vectis includes special boxes made for Ford and British Leyland. The red MG Maestro was the BL special colour; standard Corgis were yellow. The Triumph Aclaim and Mini Metro were also given away by BL at their official launches. Note also the skidmark logo of the 1984–89 management buyout Corgi company Zodiac and the fourth incarnation post-Mattel recent Corgi Vauxhall gift set.

Late in 1982, London Transport wished to order at least 5,000 Corgi #469 Routemaster buses in special liveries celebrating their fiftieth anniversary, for delivery in the spring of 1983. Due to concerns that Mettoy could be in liquidation prior to delivery, London Transport took the highly unusual step of commissioning PLAYART of Hong Kong to create new tooling cloning the Corgi #469 bus with some extra authentic enhanced detailing. Here is a 1983 gold PLAYART clone compared to a green 1979 London Transport exclusive Corgi #469. Ironically, PLAYART's Hong Kong factory ceased to make diecast toys in 1984 due to a collapse in demand. Both PLAYART and Pilen of Spain made superb copies of Corgi toys during the 1970s.

Did You Know?

One of the cheapest and most numerous 1960s castings around today, the blue #226 Morris Mini Minor, has taken on a fraudulent new life as a valuable collectable since the 1980s sell-off of Corgi factory surplus parts. Never used genuine 1960s Jensens waterslide decals can be bought from toyfairs or eBay for collectors to apply themselves to create a fictional rare toy despite it being accredited as genuine in some guides and magazines. None of the fake Minis have ever come from a Danish source; however, Corgi supplied one run (at least half a dozen gross) of these #251 Hillman Imps with pale blue body, yellow seats and Jensens decals on each side exclusively to Jensens of Denmark (a leading brand of canned meats in the 1960s). As Marcel Van Cleemput knew, no other models were ever given these logos by Corgi. Danish collectors who recall buying Corgis in the 1960s are on record recalling these Jensens Imps and the #349 Mostest Minis as the only Corgi specials sold in Denmark in the 1960s.

6

What Next?

If readers of this book wish to see more amazing images of Corgi toys the best place to start is www.vectis.co.uk – simply the finest collection of Corgi diecast photos available online anywhere. There are also exclusive details from people that sold these gems in the Vectis news archive; they have probably auctioned just about every different model Corgi ever made as well as many pre-production models and factory colour trials.

Also browse www.vintagebritishdiecasts.co.uk, which is a very useful illustrated database of all big Corgi models, and some of the small Husky and Juniors too, alongside other brands made in the UK.

If readers of this book would like to see Corgi Toys of all descriptions in the metal then visit a toyfair or swapmeet locally – www.collectors-club-of-great-britain.co.uk is a toy fair and swapmeet online event calender for events throughout the UK.

Any questions readers of this book may have can be answered by experts that chat on www.facebook.com diecast toy groups – there are dozens of these which can be UK only or International. It's best to look for ones dealing with vintage toys rather than modern toys or collectables. It is possible to meet like-minded people to chat with and learn online about Corgi and rival toy car brands as well as buy from or visit local collectors.

What To Read Next?

The Great Book of Corgi 1956–1983 by Marcel Van Cleemput (New Cavendish Books) ISBN 1-872727-19-0 Probably the greatest book ever written about any toy brand and superbly illustrated – there is nothing of any significance about the history of big Corgis that isn't included in the first and second editions (the third edition has been revised and isn't as informative).

Corgi Juniors & Husky Models: A Complete Identification and Price Guide by Bill Manzke (Schiffer Books) ISBN 0-7643-1951-5 This is the only detailed book so far published about the Husky, Rockets and Corgi Juniors small 3-inch Corgi cars – it is a well researched book with fine photos.

Ramsay's British Diecast Model Toys Catalogue (Swapmeet Publications) ISBN 0-9528352-6-6 All or any editions have a near-complete checklist of every single Corgi ever made with a reasonable estimated value at publication date – excellent to carry around when out buying old toy cars!

Corgi Toys by Dr Edward Force (Schiffer Books) ISBN 0-7643-0253-1 The late Dr Ed Force collected Corgi Toys when they were brand new in shops worldwide and wrote about them before the Internet and before anybody else well informed. This book features good profile photos of each Corgi main casting, big and small, presented from the perspective of a man who knew the whole range when it was current and was never fooled by eBay market collector-made fake variations using original 1960s and 1970s decals, stickers and parts sold off when Mettoy was liquidated.

What To Collect Next?

Try to focus your collecting on quality over quantity and try to limit yourself to items that you really really like – perhaps there is enough nostalgia for many at minimal cost in collecting original Corgi collector or dealer catalogues from 1957 to 1983, combined with a virtual collection of Corgi Toys photographs from vectis.co.uk and other sites on the Internet. Corgi made a thousand different models which came in multiple different colours that can be collected digitally for just a few seconds of time each.

For those who wish to buy Corgis, first decide whether mint-and-boxed, the charm of playworn cars or toys somewhere in between is what warms your heart and suits your pocket. Create a sustainable hobby with each Corgi toy you own becoming a personal ray of sunshine from simpler childhood times (rather than a passing fad that drowns your enthusiasm with hundreds of not-so-special old toys). Learn your way around the range at vectis.co.uk and look at auction photographs to work out which Corgis you like best before buying as well as getting an idea of their likely cost and market value. Don't expect to make a profit re-selling Corgi Toys. Profits are only easy to make when bulk-buying good collections that haven't been compromised by restorations or reproductions or fakes. When paying a significant price for any Corgi, research its value and correct factory appearance before buying to avoid overpaying or being cheated. It can become an obsessive hobby for those falling into the trap of trying to collect all Corgi Toys!

Collect a selection of Corgi catalogues for their artwork, which includes some pre-production and colour trial models which differ from the final products.

Please take note how easy it is to fake your own rare collectable red spot wheeled Whizzwheel model like this Rolls-Royce because wheels are easily levered off axles, leaving minimal traces – it's wise to avoid paying premiums for any Corgi with standard paint but uncommon wheels.

Repainting and customising your own old Corgi Toys is a fine hobby for those who like using paints. Good quality spare parts can be purchased from suppliers like Steve Flowers at www.model-supplies.co.uk.

Corgi Toys have been modified, faked, restored and customised by their owners over the decades – it is a significant profitable hobby business, as eBay.com attests. The highest quality workmanship commands prices that reflect the labour and materials that have gone into making these works of art, often to a specific order. Due to the very limited demand, the resale values of these can be problematic.

Unscrupulous or sometimes downright ignorant sellers sell a lot of so called 'rare' Corgi Toys on eBay, implying that they are factory originals when in fact they are common toys that feature home-made alterations that render them fraudulent if sold as genuine originals. Learn how to spot genuine Corgi factory finished toys and boxes to avoid being swindled by fakes, recreations and restorations – newly made boxes in particular can be so well made today that telling them apart from the originals needs a magnifying glass not a photograph!

Where To Buy Vintage Corgi Toys

www.vectis.co.uk for high-end mint boxed and genuine factory special trial products.

www.ebay.com for common models and customised toys, but beware of sellers selling fakes and customs passed off as originals.

www.facebook.com – buy from other collectors that you can get to know first from British diecast and Corgi chat groups.

Toyfairs, antique shops and fleamarkets – search for dates online